To Leo River
Enjoy!

THE MOON THE STARS & FAST CARS

by Sharika K. Forde

Illustrator
Cameron Wilson

The Moon, The Stars & Fast Cars
Published by Watersprings Publishing,
a division of Watersprings Media House, LLC.
P.O. Box 1284 Olive Branch, MS 38654
www.waterspringsmedia.com

Contact publisher for bulk orders and permission requests.

Copyright © 2021 by Sharika K Forde. All rights reserved.

No part of this publication may be reproduced, distributed, or transmitted in any form or by any means, including photocopying, recording, or other electronic or mechanical methods, without the prior written permission of the publisher, except in the case of brief quotations embodied in critical reviews and certain other noncommercial uses permitted by copyright law.

Printed in the United States of America.
ISBN-13: 978-1-948877-93-0

Inspired by my grandson Jamir.

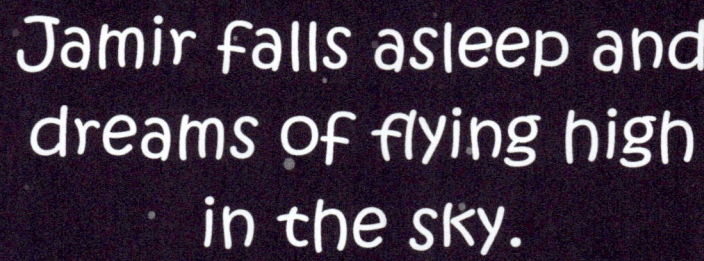

Jamir falls asleep and dreams of flying high in the sky.

He lands on the moon and the air is filled with stars.

Then a car zooms by that catches his eye.

It's red and shines so bright.

So bright that Jamir has to wear sunglasses at night.

The stop sign halted the car in its tracks.

Then more cars appeared, all lined up back to back.

They circled around the galaxy taking in all the views.

First to Saturn, Pluto and Jupiter then the cars parked on the moon.

They watched the Big Dipper, it was a mighty sight.

It was late, so the cars decided to take one last ride.

They looped around the globe with their headlights beaming high.

Then the cars honked their horns as Jamir smiled and waved goodnight.

The End

CPSIA information can be obtained
at www.ICGtesting.com
Printed in the USA
LVHW071915301021
701742LV00001B/6